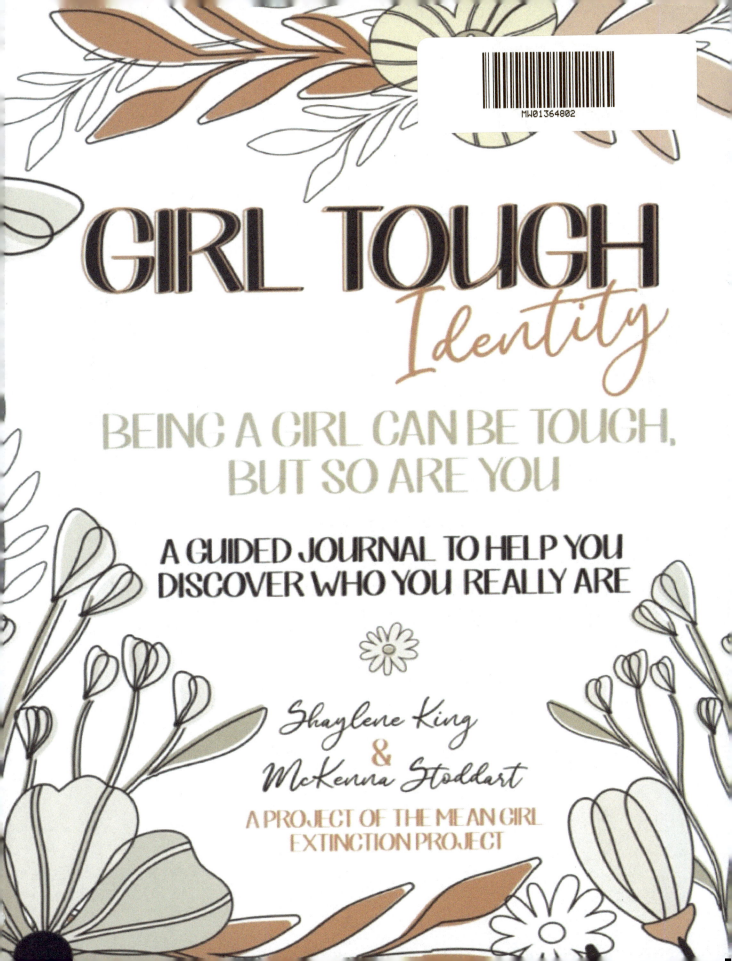

this book belongs to:

Dedicated to:

Every girl who has ever questioned who they are, this is for you.

Copyright © 2022 Shaylene King, Mckenna Stoddart and The Mean Girl Extinction Project

All rights reserved. No part of this book may be used or reproduced by any means, graphic, electronic, mechanical, including photocopying, recording, taping or by any information storage retrieval system without the written permission of the authors except in the case of brief quotations embodied in articles or reviews.

ISBN: 979-8-9856966-0-8

Library of Congress: 2022902056

Published by The Mean Girl Extinction Project

For information on bulk purchases please email shaylene@tmgep.com.

The Mean Girl Extinction Project
PO Box 632
Morgan Hill, CA 95039
tmgep.com

Cultivating kindness in girl world.

Table of Contents

SECTION ONE: Who Are You?

Chapter One:
Family & Culture (Page 13)

Chapter Two:
Friends (Page 23)

Chapter Three:
Gender Identity (Page 33)

Chapter Four:
Beliefs (Page 43)

Chapter Five:
Self (Page 53)

SECTION TWO: Change

Chapter Six:
Outside (Page 70)

Chapter Seven:
Inside (Page 81)

SECTION THREE: Insecurity

Chapter Eight:
Insecurity (Page 97)

Chapter Nine:
Prejudice (Page 107)

Chapter Ten:
Spark Confidence (Page 115)

SECTION FOUR: Competition

Chapter Eleven:
Competition & Comparison (Page 129)

Chapter Twelve:
Social Media (Page 143)

SECTION FIVE: Celebration

Chapter Thirteen:
YOU DID IT! (Page 157)

Before You Jump In

{a guide to success for the journal}

" A Little Note from us:

We know that being a girl and navigating girl world can be tough, so we're here to help. The goal of this journal is to guide you to develop a better understanding of who YOU are, create positive health around your identity so you can be a part of a movement of girls supporting girls, and create a better girl world for everyone to live in!

The pages of this journal are dressed with flowers as a constant reminder of the growth and bloom that happens when we put down our roots in healthy soil!

Our desire is to create safety and new learning. We hope you experience our love for you through the pages of this journal.

Shaylene King, Mckenna Stoddart, and The Mean Girl Extinction Project Team

"

TOP TIPS:

1. HEADINGS

Understand that each chapter is sectioned under four different headings, each with its own kind of theme and purpose.

Let's talk about it

This heading will kick off each chapter, giving you the information we will tackle. Just read this part and let it soak in.

GET INTO IT

This second heading is designed to activate what you just read. Here you will practice activities that will connect you to what you learned.

Go Deeper

In the third heading you will process what you have practiced. This is the journaling section. We invite you to look inside and dig deep.

You go girl

This last heading is a to-do list!
Try out as many of the challenges as you can!

2. UNLEASH YOUR CREATIVE SIDE

We designed this journal with lots of intentional places for you to make this journal your own. Take art breaks, color in the black and white, scribble in the margins, learn the power of art for expression, and leave your mark throughout these pages.

3. BE REAL

To get the most out of this journal, it's important to be honest with yourself: the good, bad, happy and sad. This is a journey of discovery. Express your emotions and feelings – this journal is between you and yourself only. Allow yourself time to process, unwind and care for yourself.

YOU ARE READY!

> We are so excited you are here and taking the time to invest in yourself.
>
> One last reminder. You are not alone. If these chapters bring up pain for you, please reach out. We have included resources at the back of the journal to encourage you and offer extra support as you navigate girl world. We know being a girl is tough, but so are you!
>
> love,
> *Shaylene + Mckenna*
>
> *& your friends at The Mean Girl Extinction Project*

SECTION ONE

Who Are You?

Together we are diving into what makes you, YOU. We will look at five chapters for a deep dive into knowing yourself: family & culture, friends, gender identity, beliefs and self.

"YOUR STORY IS IMPORTANT"

Before you hop into the chapters, take a moment to relax, and try this activity on the next page

Who Are You Really?

Take **one color** and write inside the portrait phrases & words describing who you see yourself to be - this could be a sport you participate in, physical features you have, or anything that relates to how you see yourself.

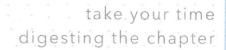
take your time digesting the chapter

CHAPTER ONE

Family & Culture

Let's talk about it

Who are you? Not sure? Let me help a sister out! Who you are includes your beliefs, looks, personality, behaviors, expressions and opinions. They create your identity. And your identity is everything that's uniquely YOU! Many things impact who you are today: your past, environment, friends, culture, family (or lack thereof). What you are taught and told impacts the way you think and how you see yourselves and others.

When I was growing up, my family made a recipe called "grandma's overnight sweet buns." During Thanksgiving and Christmas, we put on our aprons and devoted an entire day to the making of these sweet dinner buns.

As a small girl, I tried to make sense of the tattered handwritten recipe card, which had multiple handwritings and was filled with notes and scribbles. This incredibly long baking process bonded my family, but, to be honest, some years I wished we could skip over the whole experience and simply buy pre-made sweet Hawaiian bread rolls like other families.

Over time, however, I realized this process was sort of a family ritual. After all, the recipe had been passed down in our family for nearly 100 years! When this began to matter to me, it changed my view of the recipe, and I took pride in this tradition. It's a tradition I now love and plan to pass down in my family.

There is richness in tradition - to learn what we can from our culture and family can help us better understand ourselves. We learn how to be the type of person we want to become (or don't want to become) from our caregivers and others we have grown up around. Where we come from impacts how we see ourselves and the world around us. Yes, we still write our own stories. As women, it is important to look back and decide what aspects, traditions, and characteristics "fit" for us and what we will take with us into our future.

We are not our upbringing, but there is much to be gained and learned about how our family, culture and environment have influenced who we are and who we want to be. Your story is powerful. Telling and celebrating your story impacts you and your community. What you take with you is YOUR choice. You choose how your past will influence your future.

Your middle/high school years will greatly impact your identity. Where were you born? What's your family tree? What do you like about your culture, race, ethnicity, gender? What are some traditions/rituals you'd like to carry with you or steal from another's upbringing?

Questions like these will help you unpack the past and process your unique combination of family and culture– to celebrate it and even learn something new!

- Mckenna

GET INTO IT

> to soak in what you read, try these activities

Mirror

Below, capture 3 of your favorite traits/aspects about your family or racial culture. Once you have written these down, go write them on a mirror near you! To do this, find a sticky note, a piece of paper you can tape up, or a whiteboard marker you can use to decorate your mirror!

1. _____

2. _____

3. _____

Recipe

Brainstorm something positive that either has been passed down from your upbringing or a new tradition you'd like to start! (Like a recipe, a get-together, a funny dance when a certain song comes on, a holiday tradition, etc.) Capture this special idea in the space below.

Recipe: Pers:

Ingredients: Directions:

Family Tree

Create a diagram of your history so you can visually see patterns about your upbringing thus far (like names being passed down, traditions, beliefs, values, occupations, interests, hobbies, languages etc.) For some, this may look like a family tree. For others, it may be less rigid, like you in the middle with other factors in your past captured by certain shapes/colors to best show any patterns.

here are some questions to help you dig deep.

1. What is one of your favorite lessons that you have learned from an adult/mentor in your life?

2. What is a favorite "tradition" of yours? Yes, this could be something you started yourself!

3. If you learned a little from the family tree about generations before you, capture some cool traditions from your culture. Whatever continent you are originally from, look into traditions that connect you to your past! If you aren't sure about your family history, take a look into cultural traditions that interest you!

4. How has your upbringing/family influenced who you are? How has having siblings (or not) shaped you?

You go girl

try out these challenges this week!

- ☐ Share the tradition you want to continue (or the one you want to start!) with a friend!

- ☐ Which family member or someone you admire do you look the most like? Dress up like them and recreate an old photo!

- ☐ If you enjoy music, research and learn a song/national anthem, that can be a source of pride from your history, family, culture, beliefs or other traditions.

CHAPTER TWO
Friends

Let's talk about it

Did you know the friends you choose can hugely influence the person you become? They can impact your values, affect your attitudes and influence the decisions you make. So, it goes without saying… (but I'll say it anyway), it's super important to choose your friends wisely!

My cheer coach once said, "Tell me who your friends are, and I will tell you who you are." Her point was this: if you choose friends who are kind, inclusive and encouraging, you will likely also be kind, inclusive and encouraging.

But the same can also be true… if your friends are insecure, unkind and gossipers, you will probably find yourself to be insecure, unkind and a gossip. Funny how that works, huh? Unfortunately, I learned this the hard way. In middle school, I traded my two good friends to be part of the "cool" crowd. THE. WORST. YEAR. EVER! My new friends were toxic. Gossiping, backstabbing and girl drama were rampant, and I fully participated in all of it. By summer, I had developed low self-esteem, poor body image, and my insecurity was off the hook. I went from being happy and positive to negative, angry and untrusting. What changed? The answer is simple. When you spend time with your friends, their behavior, values and attitudes can rub off on you. The question is, what's actually rubbing off on you? Does it positively or negatively influence you?

The truth is, friends will influence you. The good news is - YOU get to decide who your friends are and just HOW they will influence you.

-Shaylene

GET INTO IT

Thermometer - *Friendship Quiz*

What is the temperature of your friendships? Are they healthy or unhealthy?

Think of your friend group, or a close friend. Go through the list of healthy/unhealthy characteristics. For each true characteristic about your friendship/(s) write the characteristic on the line next to the correct thermometer, then color in the thermometer. Which thermometer is higher? What do you think these thermometers say about the health of your friendships? Notice the characteristics you filled in for both thermometers. What needs to continue, what needs to change?

Healthy Relationship	Unhealthy Relationship
Accepting of you	Criticizing/Degrading
You can express yourself freely	You feel scared to express yourself
Compliments others	Makes fun of others
Honest	Lies
Kind	Unkind
Speaks up when something's wrong	Cares only about themselves
Authentic	Fake
Laughs with you	Laughs at you
Upfront	Manipulative
Avoids drama	Creates drama

Healthy Relationships

Unhealthy Relationships

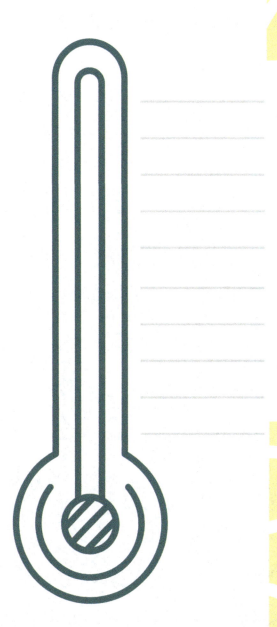

Friendship Venn Diagram

Have you ever wondered why you are friends with someone? Maybe it's because of something you have in common or perhaps it's because you're so different! Sometimes it can help to see things laid out in front of you. Compare yourself to a friend.

In the top circle put your friend's name. Put your name in the bottom circle.

List each of your unique qualities in the individual circles, then in the middle, capture your similarities.

What do you have in common? How are you different? How do your unique individual qualities affect your friendship?

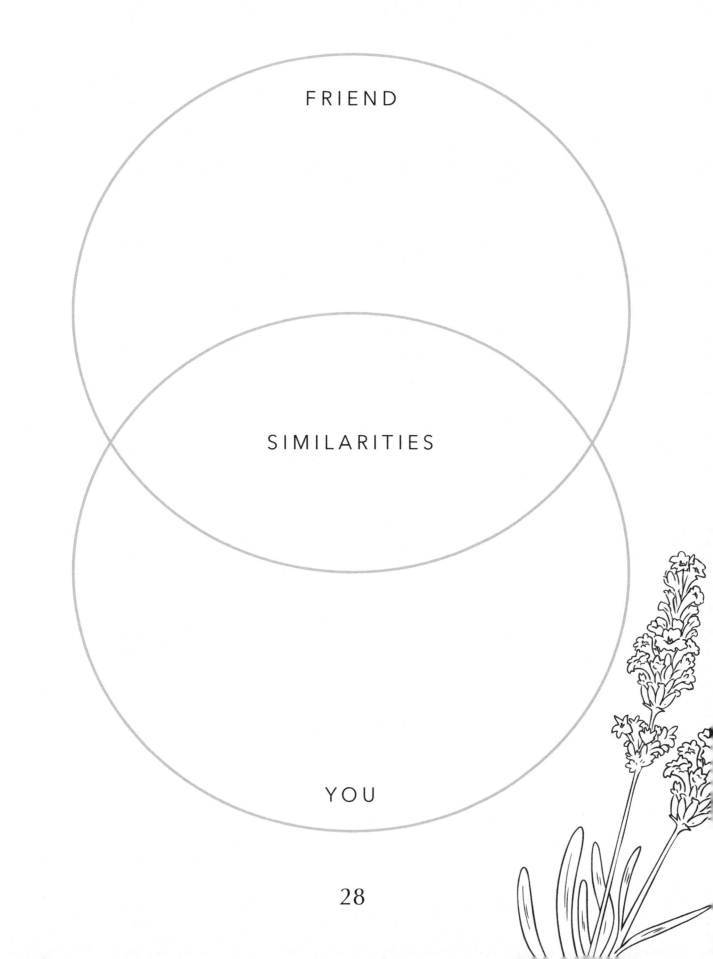

1. Look at yourself in the mirror. What kind of friend is staring back at you? How can you be a better friend?

2. Write about the history of one of your friendships. Include: How did you meet, why did you choose them as a friend, what do you do for fun, how do you resolve conflicts, and what do you wish for your friendship?

3. Refer to your Friendship Thermometer exercise - let's unpack it. Do you have any negative friendships in your life right now that you realize are not good for you? What is it that makes them unhealthy for you? Are they worth saving? Or do you need to think about letting them go?

You go girl

- [ ] July 30th is International Friendship Day! Send a card "old school" through the mail to your friends and tell them what you appreciate about them.

- [ ] Create a positive song playlist specifically for you and your friends and share it with them.

- [ ] Go out of your way this week to be a good friend. Send an encouraging text, surprise your friend with their favorite candy bar, drop a note in their locker or pick something else you know would make your friend's day!

CHAPTER THREE
Gender Identity

Let's talk about it

What do you think of when I say pink or blue? Do you think girl or boy? If you did, it's probably because you've been taught the colors pink and blue identify the gender of girl and boy. Next time you're in a store (like Target or Walmart), go check out the toy aisles. Was it difficult to see what toys were geared toward girls? Let me guess - you saw lots of pink and glitter? This is an example of gender roles. What are gender roles? I'm glad you asked! They're expectations society puts on us. Gender roles tell us how males and females "should'' act, dress, speak and conduct themselves. Unfortunately, gender stereotypes can cause discrimination, and the person using them might not even realize they're doing it!!

For example, boys are taught they shouldn't cry, must be tough, fight to stand up for themselves (or others), should enjoy sports, cars/trucks/motorcycles, action movies/video games, and the list goes on. This is a lot of pressure to put on boys. They have real feelings (just like girls do) and can't possibly live up to all of these expectations without experiencing negative consequences.

Similarly, as a girl, we grow up with messages saying we should be skinny, mothering, submissive, accommodating, need to be taken care of/protected, always look good, know how to cook, and should even be embarrassed for having our period.

Where do you get these messages? TV, movies, video games, news, people you hang around, and even retail stores!

Gender roles can confine us to only a "female" box or a "male" box. But really, who likes to be told what box they should be in? What about the boy who is in touch with his emotions and maybe doesn't like sports? Perhaps he becomes a musician, artist, social worker or the next Mr. Rogers - all of which we need in this world! Did you know that football players actually become better players when they learn ballet? But the boy who wants to take ballet classes will surely be made fun of or called names.

What about the girl who loves sports? Or digs math & science and maybe doesn't dream of having children? Perhaps she's a tomboy and wants to be a cop, firefighter, engineer, or professional athlete! All of which we need in this world!

The bottom line is this - don't let others tell you who/what you should be or that you can't follow your dreams or pursue your interests because of your anatomy or gender identity.

- Shaylene &
The Mean Girl Extinction Project team

> Women are like teabags. We don't know our true strength until we are in hot water.
>
> – ELEANOR ROOSEVELT

GET INTO IT

Check your Boxes

Create your own box. No "female" or "male" box. What fits in yours? For example: maybe you like having short hair, skateboarding and/or you love gaming – things considered male stereotypes. Put these kinds of things in the box that fits you. Female stereotypes might be: being flirtatious, emotional or naive. If these are not you, put them in the other box!

My box, here's what fits for me!

```


```

The other box that I don't fit in!

```


```

Movie Time!

Watch some movies that include females living outside of the "female" box. Here are some examples: Hidden Figures, League of their Own, Brave, Danghal, Mulan and Harriet.

Period.

Getting your period is as natural as having to go to the bathroom. Whenever we have to use the restroom, we need toilet paper right? So, don't be embarrassed by needing a pad or tampon. Want more information on this subject? Read the book: "Periods Gone Public" by Jennifer Weiss-Wolf.

Go Deeper

1. Have you had a "gender lightbulb moment?" (a time you became aware of being treated differently because of your gender) If so, what was it and how did this experience influence you? Did it change how/what you wanted to do?

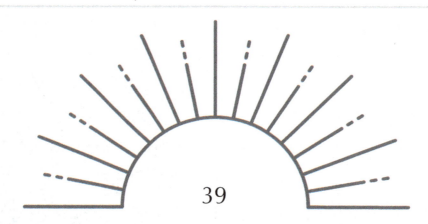

2. Have you noticed yourself gender stereotyping? What can you do to change the narrative?

3. How has society's stereotypes/expectations impacted you?

You go girl

- [ ] Take notice and encourage others for stepping outside of their gender roles. When a boy expresses true feelings, support him. OR when a girl is competitive and wants to play typically "guy" types of games, encourage her!

- [ ] Is there something you've wanted to do but felt "boxed" in? Step out of that box!

CHAPTER FOUR

Beliefs

Let's talk about it

Do you believe in what you cannot see? As kids, we most definitely believed in what we had never seen before. Every holiday season, there is some type of character, myth, or legend that brings cheer, leaving every child smiling from ear to ear! We believed we had faith, because we wanted hope! We hoped for presents, surprise, excitement and joy…. Then we grew up…

Believing in these characters only lasts until someone ruins the illusion (hopefully, that wasn't just me ruining it for you now!! :) We know these traditions are meant to keep childlike excitement alive, like a bit of MAGIC! And in reality, these stories teach us a lot about faith because we believed in something we could not prove. What keeps you believing in something you can't see? How does believing affect you?

Take love, for instance. We cannot touch it, see it, smell it, or measure it, yet we believe in it. We make decisions in its name - we crave it; we fight for it; we go crazy for it. All for something that is, in itself, intangible to us. The belief of love is turned into actions that we can see/feel, while love itself is something that's invisible.

I was raised in a family that prioritized teaching me about faith and believing in a higher power, something bigger than myself. Myths like Santa Claus actually taught me a lot, even if I don't still believe he shimmies down my fake chimney. I learned that my faith in something I do believe in is powerful. It can help me make decisions, love others well, give me direction and offer hope! It changed my life and has become my "north" on the compass that guides who I am. Believing in a higher power took a weight off my shoulders, giving my life more purpose. My world is not just about M-E.

As we care for ourselves, and as we take a moment to slow down, reflect, and explore, it is important to give attention, time, and energy to our spiritual health. Your spirituality can be key to who you are, guiding you through your convictions, values and morals.

When we go against what we believe, we can create tension within ourselves which is why it is important to nurture our spiritual health.

How do we nurture spiritual health? It will look different for everyone. For me, it can often look like prayer, silence, or journaling. For you, it may look like time in nature, singing, writing, dancing - the list goes on. Why does it matter? Knowing what we believe helps us understand ourselves on a deeper level. When we find ourselves in hard times, our belief is often what helps us come home to ourselves and remember who we are.

Throughout your culture, have you been brought up, like I was, with faith? Was this something you learned about, or is this a new concept for you? I encourage you to take some time to review these questions and be honest with your answers.

- Mckenna

GET INTO IT

Check in with Yourself

Take 30 minutes to measure your spiritual temperature, slow down and just be one with yourself, first by creating a relaxing environment (a clean, quiet enjoyable space that smells good for you to experience peace).

Here are some ideas to get you started: journaling, yoga, prayer, dance, art, reading sacred text, a walk in nature, meditation.

Once you have completed an activity, "check in" and capture your thoughts in the space below. How did you feel before the activity vs. after?

_____

_____

_____

_____

_____

_____

Moral Compass

Take a moment to fill in the compass with your "north."

At the top (where North would normally go), place your guiding principle. This is how you ultimately make decisions - based on your main priority, your belief system. For example, how do you know when something is right or wrong? What do you believe in that's most important to you?

At the other points on the compass, capture additional values, beliefs, and morals that guide you in life, making you "who you are."

1. What can you do to best care for your own soul?

2. Describe below how you are in touch with your own thoughts & beliefs (not just the thoughts/beliefs of those around you).

3. When you wake up in the morning, what brings you hope? What motivates and drives you?

4. Like love, wind is another example of what we know exists, but cannot see. What is something you can feel, but you have never laid eyes on?

You go girl

- ☐ During the next few days, consider and make a list of all the things you believe in that you don't/can't see.

- ☐ Ask your closest friend what they believe in, be a good listener and discover what you can learn.

> You never know how much you really believe anything until its truth or falsehood becomes a matter of life and death to you.
> -- C. S. Lewis

CHAPTER FIVE
Self

Let's talk about it

When we ask the question, "who am I?" we have to get really honest with ourselves. We are asking, what makes me...ME? As we have talked about, so much of who we are can be affected by our family and culture, who we choose as friends, how we express our femininity, and what we believe in. As much as those influences all can play a part, in the end, we decide who we are, and true confidence comes from knowing the answer to that very question. Who do I know myself to be? How do I wish to be? What would I like to create and fill my world with?

In other words, what is the good/positive to keep with you and take forward? What is the bad/negative that can be left behind? Growing up is a process. It is important to feel safe - to try to explore these ideas, as you discover who you are.

We all have the choice, and our choices might change over time. Who you are this year might look different than who you were last year - and maybe even more different than who you will become next year.

Your personality is also what makes you-YOU. Perhaps you're like me, obsessed with taking personality tests to help you figure out who you are, or maybe a personality test isn't even something that has crossed your mind. Personality is unique to each person. We all have different strengths and gifts we bring to the world. Figuring out who you are by nature and who you choose to be is key in "knowing yourself." You will discover you have the ability to choose how you will be impacted by your culture, family, friends, and outside influences like social media. What things do you do that are uniquely "you?" What have you been told about yourself all your life? Do these statements seem to "fit" you?

Everyone is on their own adventure of discovering themselves, and it actually never stops. The journey, while having many highs, will also include some lows. It is important to learn from both. In gracefully attempting to embrace what comes our way, we can lean into a process called radical acceptance. Radical acceptance is an exercise and mindset we will learn together, where we can find peace and the ability to move through the lows that affect us. It is so important to be honest about what is and has gone on in our lives, and to celebrate who we are now. Let's look into some ways to reflect on YOU!

-Mckenna

GET INTO IT

What's in a Name?

Write down your name. Look up its meaning online, and decide what it means to you. You can also reflect on any nicknames and how it feels when someone calls you by them.

_____
_____
_____
_____
_____

Take a Personality Test!

As we mentioned previously, your personality is changing in these years- it's not set in stone. That being said, there are tools that can help you understand where your personality is right now. These tools are not meant to place you in a box, but to give you the language to explore how you feel/respond and how your personality and strengths might be experienced by others.

You can use the website: Truity.com and research which test could be helpful to take. Other examples include Enneagram, Myers-Briggs, Strengths Finders, DISC. Before you take a test, make sure you talk to your parents or guardian so they can help you!

Radical Acceptance

Everyone comes from different backgrounds/ experiences. Maybe as you were reading or processing the information in this section, some feelings and memories have come up for you (after all, memories and feelings go hand in hand). Maybe there have been moments in your life of injustice and pain done to you (the bad you want to leave behind). If so, there is an exercise you may find helpful to experience some peace over such circumstances in your life. Radical Acceptance is a therapy strategy used in Dialectical Behavior Therapy (DBT), but this kind of practice is a tool anyone can use. You do not have to face any problem alone. Through the TMGEP website, you can find a video where Mckenna will lead you through the process. There are also helplines at the back of the journal if you need someone to reach out to.

What is radical acceptance? It is completely and fully accepting the things that have happened to you, in your life, at a deep heart level. Instead of ignoring what is irritating or hurting you, accepting it can help you move forward. Acceptance like this helped me when my grandma passed away very suddenly a few years ago. It was unexpected, and I felt it was unfair, but there was nothing I could do to change it. I just needed to fully accept the reality and find the peace to move on. You can use this tool with any situation, big or small, to settle the issue within your heart.

How can I practice this exercise? First, relax your mind and body, take deep breaths, close your eyes, and shut all thoughts out of your mind to focus on your breath. When you are ready, bring up a moment of hurt or pain in your past that still comes up for you. A moment that, however big or small, has mattered to you, and still manages to sting you when it can. When you are ready, follow the prompts of the exercise.

- **Observe** what you are struggling with, fighting with reality: "but it shouldn't be this way!"/ "it shouldn't have happened".

- **Remind yourself** that reality can't be changed. This is what happened. Everyone's life is built on their own series of events.

- **Practice accepting** with your heart, soul, mind and body. Place your hands facing up to release your control over what has happened. Let your face turn into a half-smile as you focus on deep breathing and acceptance.

- **Move forward** in your language around this event. Say (out loud) the things you would do if you accepted the facts, and believe that you have already done it!

- **Allow yourself** to feel the emotions that arise. Radical acceptance is not about saying what happened was "ok". It is about knowing that to move forward and have peace, you have to accept what has happened and continue to take steps forward

- **Repeat** this process of "self-talk" until you are ready to accept reality as it is and not let that pain from your past rule over your present. As the pain may surely try to take the reins again, come back to this exercise and give yourself grace as you practice a new skill/mindset.

Go Deeper

1. What is one of your favorite characteristics about yourself?

2. How would you describe your "vibe"? How do you think others would describe your vibe?

3. What is something you wish you could change about yourself?

4. What is a compliment you have been given that you often think about?

You go girl

- [ ] Think deep. Come up with a compliment you can give someone about who they are on the inside, then tell that person and make their day! Sometimes, people struggle to accept compliments, but let's never stop giving them!

- [ ] Wear an outfit this week that embodies who you are, ask a friend to join you.

☐ Flip back to the beginning of "Who am I?" (page 12) and find the self portrait you did, with all the words about yourself. With a different color go back and add more detail, fill your picture with any new thoughts you gained in this chapter!

☐ Design your own logo, something you can create that would tell others about you! Research whether you can make that logo into a sticker! (Find a DIY video on youtube that can walk you through how to do it at home!)

SECTION TWO

Change

Let's dive into change together. These years are full of changes for you, so let's come up with some helpful tactics to navigate all the transitions in your life.

"CHOOSE KIND INCLUSIVE ENCOURAGING FRIENDS & YOU WILL LIKELY BECOME KIND INCLUSIVE & ENCOURAGING."

"Well, I must endure the presence of a few caterpillars if I wish to become acquainted with the butterflies."
— Antoine de Saint-Exupéry

CHAPTER SIX

Outside

Let's talk about it

When I was your age, I was a planner. I liked to know what I was doing, when I was doing it, and then plan accordingly. I thrived in environments I could control. Basically, order, predictability, and I were BFF's. But then a frenemy showed up and ruined everything - her name was CHANGE. Change turned my world upside down. My life went from cool, calm, and collected to out of control, unorganized, and chaotic. What happened? High School happened.

I tried out for the cheer team my freshman year and didn't make it, but all my friends did. My boyfriend cheated and broke up with me, a friend was killed in a motorcycle accident, and I was hit by a drunk driver.

Circumstances quickly went from familiar to unfamiliar, known to unknown, same to different, beginning to ending. The only common denominator was the fact they were all changes I couldn't control.

Change is unavoidable - it's a part of life. Some changes you CAN control, like how you treat people, your own attitude, thoughts, and actions. And, there are some changes you can't control, like what other people think, do, feel or say. Not being in control can leave you feeling very out of control. Maybe your parents are getting divorced, you have to move and attend a new school, or a friend doesn't want to be friends anymore. Maybe you are experiencing a disability that is a new transition, or someone you really care about has passed away.

All change requires adjustment—even good change. How do you cope with these external changes? Focus on what you CAN control!

1. **Acknowledge your emotions**. If you're angry, be angry, sad, go ahead and cry. If it's a change you're excited about but unsure of the outcome, acknowledge those feelings too. Journal, talk to a friend, or reach out to an adult you trust.

2. **Reflect** back over a change that was hard, but you successfully managed to overcome. Are you moving to a new school and worried about making friends? Reflect back to when you started your current school. How did you make the friends you have now?

3. **Alter your perspective**. Instead of looking at all the negative aspects of your circumstances, what potential positives can you take away? You might have to go between two homes now that your parents are divorced, and that might really suck. Is home life now more peaceful? Do you get more one-on-one time now with each parent?

4. **Practice self- compassion**. Give yourself a break. Change can cause stress, resentment, disappointment, and frustration - all of which can lead to self-doubt. Offer yourself some grace. Let yourself feel your emotions and pain.

GET INTO IT

My Plan of Attack for Change

We can't always control change, BUT we can control HOW we respond to it. Create a plan to help guide you through the changes that will come.

For example: If I'm feeling insecure and not liking the way I look because I'm bloated from being on my period, instead of hating on myself and eating a full pint of ice cream and wallowing in my own self-pity, my plan of attack might be:

> Alter my perspective about periods; I know I'm gonna bloat once a month. I can't change that. Practice self-acceptance. I will look forward to buying a cup of my favorite ice cream to eat, not binge on a pint in one day out of frustration.

Plan of Attack:

Control Wheel of Change

Check out the control wheel of change. What would you add to this wheel to help you "roll" through change better?

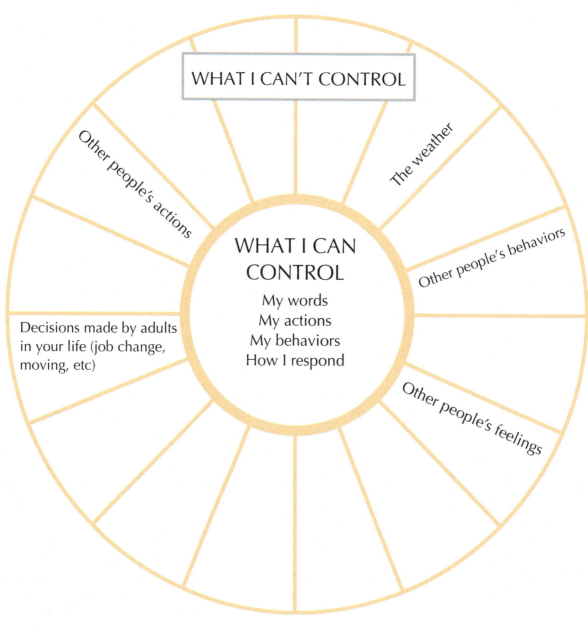

Go Deeper

1. Name a change you are usually good at handling. Describe how you learned to manage this.

2. Reflect on a change you initially thought would be all bad, but as it turns out something positive came from it. What did this experience teach you?

3. What is one thing you'd like to keep the same forever? Why?

4. What is one change in your life you would like to make? Why?

5. Why is learning to handle change important?

You go girl

- [ ] Write a letter you would send a friend to encourage them when they are going through a hard time. Put it in an envelope, address it, add a stamp and then send it to yourself! Keep it and only open it should you need it! Don't have a stamp or envelope on hand? Send it as a text or email.

- [ ] Write a list of positive thoughts and affirmations. Make it wallpaper for your phone, your computer screensaver or post it somewhere you will see it often.

- [ ] Find an inspiring quote that is meaningful to you around the topic of change, write it down and memorize it. Here is one I found by Leo Tolstoy:

"Everyone thinks of changing the world, but no one thinks of changing himself"

-Leo Tolstoy

CHAPTER SEVEN

Inside

Let's talk about it

"Life is like underwear; change is good." Funny, but true! For teenagers, change is no stranger. Whether you notice it or not, you are constantly faced with change: outside of you, in your home life, school life, friend groups, churches, sports, and family life. You are surrounded by what is not set in stone which can easily affect you. The beauty about change is that we are still in control of how we react to it, and we can choose to hop off of the emotional roller coaster change loves to take us on.

While there are many changes outside of you, I am sure you know there are many changes inside of you as well, both in body and mind. While emotions are running wild, puberty hits. When I was 13 years old, I grew to the height I have remained as an adult, 5'6.

I had a huge growth spurt and did not grow much taller than that. While I had the general size of my body today, my face had much rounder cheeks, and I did not always feel beautiful or grown-up. All it took was one girl to make one negative comment (I chose to believe), and I had developed insecurity.

Paired with the changes of puberty came brain changes. Middle schoolers can be known for being emotional and a bit all over the place. This is how we grow up - new feelings and awareness become a part of the equation, and it can be A LOT to deal with!! For me, this meant that little criticisms about how I looked, or the color of my hair (being a redhead), left me stinging and sensitive. Eventually, I learned tools to understand whether people's hurtful comments were actual truths that I should consider or simply ridicule based on their own insecurity. If it was simply ridicule, I learned to not let the hurtful comments in - which took lots of work! Plus, with time, my face did thin out, and I grew into my body… some things just take a bit longer :)

Our thoughts impact our feelings and how we perceive what's happening in our lives, which can then affect our behavior. So, it is super important to check in on our thoughts and evaluate them because they may not always be true - just like a negative comment from someone else isn't necessarily true!

Part of what makes this time in your life a bit awkward is that everyone your age is changing at different rates, and it's easy to criticize ourselves and others. If there are days you feel super "off," or not yourself, just remember you are not alone. If you feel like I felt - insecure about your body, I totally get it. You are not alone. If you are wondering if your growth spurt will ever come, remember that you are right in the middle of change, and you are not alone.

Aspects of your life may feel super unsettled right now and could just need more time. During this shift and change, decide to respond to change differently than you had in the past. For example, your reaction to change has the power to increase your insecurity OR increase your strength. YOU can change your thoughts, which can change your attitude! Let's learn to be gracious with ourselves and share that grace with others.

-Mckenna

GET INTO IT

> The exercises we are about to do are tools that my mom taught me when I was your age & I still use them today.
>
> -Mckenna

The Emotional Umbrella

Picture this. Raining down on you are the words and comments people say to you. You have no control over what they say - just like you have no control over the weather or getting caught in a rainstorm. The only thing in your control is your reaction to what they say. You decide how you will prepare for a storm - will you grab an umbrella today? Choose which raindrops you let roll off your umbrella and which raindrops you reach out to grab and pull inside.

In the picture, fill in (or next to/around) the raindrops with the comments you are choosing to let roll off of you, the comments that hurt you, and the ones that aren't true. Now, in the outstretched hand of the girl, write the words/comments that people say that you choose to honor and bring inside - the ones you want to believe are true and hold dear. Add as many raindrops as needed.

Even though painful, some may be pieces of constructive criticism you would like to apply to your life.

The Thoughtful Highway

The ways you let thoughts into your mind matter. We are in charge of building healthy "thought highways" in our minds. Sometimes negative comments build up inside us and instead create a "highway to destruction," a thought process leading us down a negative path. When you notice this happening in your mind, it's time to build a new highway, a "highway to health." (Highways aren't built overnight; to rebuild and re-route, give yourself grace in the midst of your roadwork).

In this exercise, fill in what your "highway to destruction" can look like and what the negative thoughts appear like in your mind. Now, capture your thoughts and re-route them down your "highway to health." Fill that highway with the healthy thoughts that permeate you with joy and confidence (if there is not enough space to fill your words on the highway, write them next to the road).

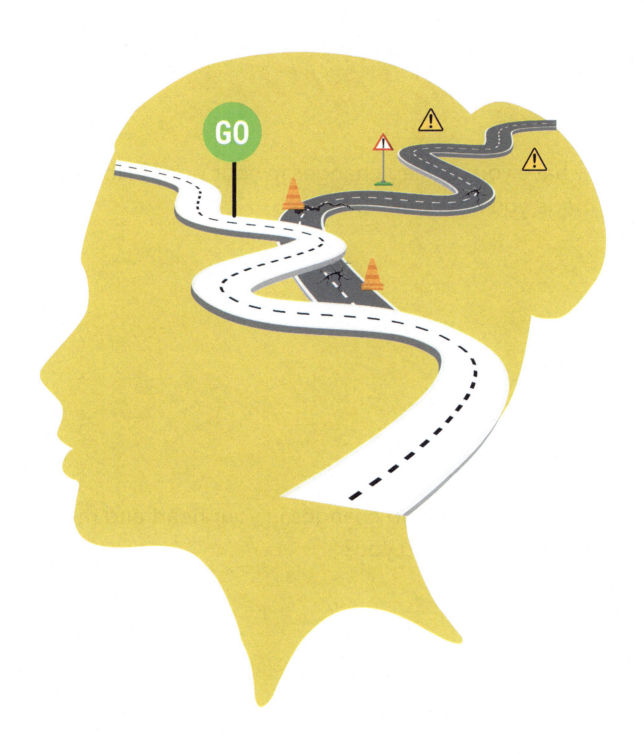

Go Deeper

1. How have you noticed changes in your body? How have they made you feel?

2. How have you noticed changes in your heart and mind? How have they affected you?

3. Have you found yourself comparing how you have changed to how others have changed? Why/why not?

You go girl

- [ ] Take a moment to draw an umbrella - wherever you capture reminders. You could write it on your hand, in your phone notes, on a sticky note on your bedroom door. Keep this image with you today, and when someone says something you do not believe is true about you, picture it rolling right off!

- [ ] Who is your favorite celebrity? Look them up online and see if you can find a picture of them at your age!

> Just when a caterpillar thought its life was over, it became a butterfly

SECTION THREE

Insecurity

Insecurity is something that all people are plagued by. Whether we realize it or not, it can rule our actions, so let's focus on some tools to radiate confidence instead!

"Belief helps us come home to ourselves."

CHAPTER EIGHT

Insecurity

Let's talk about it

I write middle-grade fiction for girls, and in one of my books, I describe the teen years as "insecure-a-TEEN." Did I just describe you? I know it described me as a teen! Research shows insecurity begins to rear its ugly head starting at the age of 9 and is at its highest from ages 12 to 17. These are the years your body begins to develop, hormones are raging out of control, and you're trying to figure out who you are and what your place is in the world.

Back in 2014, I founded The Mean Girl Extinction Project, an anti-bully organization for girls. It was created out of the need to help girls navigate relational aggression (girl bullying). After working with thousands of girls across the country, I can confidently say girl bullying is deeply rooted in insecurity: **Every. Single. Time.**

The insecurities may look different, but I'm convinced that all roads lead back to some form of insecurity. Here is a short list (but not all) of the top insecurities girls struggle with:
- self-esteem
- body image
- relationships
- sexuality
- rejection
- perfectionism
- social anxiety
- disabilities

Did you find your insecurities?

Several years ago, I was working at a school where a 13-year-old girl, Hannah (not her real name), had committed suicide. The investigation uncovered in Hannah's suicide note that a group of girls had been relentlessly bullying her. They excluded her, made fun of her, talked behind her back, spread rumors about her both in person and through social media. Hannah believed the only way she could escape the bullying was to end her life - If you ever feel this way, get help immediately, you matter. How did the bullying even start? Jealousy.

Hannah and one of the other girls (we will call her Gretchen) were part of a modeling shoot for a magazine. Hannah's picture was chosen; Gretchen's was not. Gretchen's insecurity about her looks was triggered by Hannah's picture in the magazine. Jealous, Gretchen began to mistreat Hannah. Because Gretchen was the "queen bee" of her social circle, other girls followed her lead.

This is an example of how insecurity can be used as a weapon of mass destruction if you don't learn to manage it. But guess what? You were not born insecure. Insecurity is something we learn over time from experiences, traumatic events, social conditioning, instability, and our environments (such as home and/or school). Something usually triggers insecurity. Triggers are what set us off emotionally. Do you know your triggers? You can't fix what you don't know is broken, so it's important to identify your insecurities and what triggers them. Once you do that, you can turn your triggers into transformation.

How do you handle insecurity?

1. We all have insecurities. What are you insecure about? Where does your insecurity come from? Not sure? Ask a good friend or adult you trust.

2. Identify your triggers. Learn positive self-talk to combat those triggers (we will practice this next) . Are your triggers something you see in others, yourself, or maybe both? What sets off your insecurity?

3. Face your insecurity. To defeat your insecurities, you need to name them, claim them and then confront them. When you do this, you will turn the control of power from insecurity to you.

4. Respond, don't react. When you *react* you give the insecurity control of the situation. Instead, when you *respond* instead, you are the one in control. If you usually react in anger or revenge, take a deep breath and slowly countdown from 10-1. Then, *respond* rather than *react*.

GET INTO IT

Recycle Negative Self Talk

Negative self-talk fuels insecurity. So instead, practice positive self-talk!

Grab a bag of any kind (paper, Ziploc, plastic) and write "recycle" on the bag. Separately, rip up pieces of scrap paper. On one side of the paper, write down something negative you tell yourself. Then put it in the recycle bag. Continue until you run out of negative self-talk. Close the bag and shake. Next, open the bag and pick out one piece of paper at a time. Read the negative self-talk then recycle the negative self-talk by changing it into positive self-talk. For example: (-) I wish I was shorter. (+) Because I'm tall, I can help others reach things they can't.

Don't have a bag or paper? Say them out loud to yourself.

LOVE

Learning to love ourselves will help combat insecurities and triggers, cultivating positive self-talk. Memorize **L.O.V.E.**

- **L**- Learn your good qualities and CELEBRATE them!
- **O**- Original. Be original. You do YOU sister!
- **V**- Valuable. You're never too little (or too much) and you're always enough!
- **E**- Erase. Recycle negative self-talk into positive self-talk

> **DID YOU KNOW?**
>
> It takes five compliments to counteract one put down?

1. Now that you have identified some of your triggers, how can you respond instead of react in the future?

"A flower doesn't compete with the flower next to it, it just blooms"

You go girl

- [ ] Do you know the insecurities of a friend? Make an effort this week to say or do something positive for them to help combat their insecurity. For example, if your friend struggles with insecurity about their outward appearance, give them an honest compliment on their appearance to help boost their self esteem.

- [ ] You can probably list 5 put downs you've received from others pretty easily, right? Don't write them down - we don't need to make room for them here. Instead, what about 5 compliments from others? Make room for this, and write them down here!

CHAPTER NINE

Prejudice

Let's talk about it

I love Christmas! As a child, my favorite part of Christmas was waking up in the morning to see all the wrapped gifts under the tree. My eyes immediately focused on the wrapping paper hiding the gift inside. Based on the size and shape of the wrapped gift, I would guess what my gift was before opening it. Many times, what I thought my gift was, was based on the size or shape of the box, or outside wrapping was actually not what it was on the inside. I pre-judged my gift because of what I saw on the outside.

We do the same thing with each other, don't we? We make assumptions about someone based on what we see on the outside and then pre-judge them for it. These "pre-judgments" or prejudices determine how we might treat someone. Prejudice often follows social norms.

For example, if you see someone who is disabled at school, and the social norm at your school is to ignore kids with disabilities, you might ignore them, too. Or maybe a girl at school has come out as LGBTQ+, and you see this year, she is now sporting a short haircut and wearing the same clothes as what the "boys" are wearing. If the social norm is not inclusive of the LGBTQ+ community on your campus, you would likely follow their lead. And you only need to see the headlines on newspapers or TV to know there is a lot of prejudice around race.

The truth is, we all have been pre-judged based on what we look like. We are pre-judged for our race, clothes we wear, age, our culture, sexual orientation, religion, who we hang around, size and shape of our body, gender, athlete or math-alete… the list goes on. Prejudices about you are going to play into how you see yourself. Prejudice usually leads to people being judged unfairly, which can impact their sense of self. Some of the prejudices about you might be really hard and hurtful. It impacts your identity. Don't let others' prejudices define you. Just because someone has made assumptions about you, doesn't mean they are correct.

As you work on your identity and make decisions about who you are or who you want to be, be mindful of these prejudices - both the ones you are pre-judged for and the ones you are pre-judging. Next time you notice the "wrapping" on the outside of someone, don't just make assumptions about them. Tear off the wrapping and look at what's inside that person. Learn to judge someone based on who they really are, not who you think they are from what you see.

- Shaylene

GET INTO IT

Gift Box

On the outside of the gift below, write prejudices others might have just by looking at you. On the inside of the gift, write about who you really are - what they don't see.

Check yourself.

Here is a checklist of some prejudices I mentioned earlier. Put a check in the boxes of prejudices you've had when you pre-judge others.

- ☐ Race
- ☐ Disabilities
- ☐ Age
- ☐ Culture
- ☐ Religion
- ☐ Clothes (what someone wears)
- ☐ Physical appearance (size/shape)
- ☐ Athlete
- ☐ Math-alete
- ☐ Skin color
- ☐ Gender
- ☐ Sexual orientation
- ☐ Who someone hangs around

For the boxes you checked, spend some time learning about those prejudices. You will be less likely to pre-judge or mistreat others when you know more about them, not just what you see on the outside.

Go Deeper

1. Look at the pre-judgments you wrote on the outside of the gift activity. Based on these pre-judgements, how were you treated? How did that make you feel? Did they affect how you saw yourself?

2. Now think about someone you've pre-judged. What was your first impression? How did you treat them just by looking at them? How do you think it made them feel? Why do you think you judged them the way you did?

3. What can you do moving forward to stop negative prejudice?

You go girl

- [ ] Find someone at school you have pre-judged. Make an effort to get to know them.

- [ ] Next time you meet someone new, focus more on the gift that they are to the world, and less about the wrapping paper they come in.

CHAPTER TEN
Spark Confidence

Let's talk about it

"Every great dream begins with a dreamer. Always remember, you have within you the strength, the patience, and the passion to reach for the stars to change the world."

Harriet Tubman said that. When I think of confidence, I think of Harriet. Harriet led the underground railroad, freeing slaves for 8 years. She had the strength to gain her freedom, the courage to go back, and the ability to lead others to be just as brave. She was bold, skilled, smart, and compassionate, a true pillar of confidence.

When you hear the word "confidence," who do you think of? What do you think of? What does confidence mean to you?

Have you ever seen or been a part of a group of girls looking in the mirror, all criticizing their bodies one after the other, putting themselves down? I know I have - more times than I can count, at all stages of life. Insecurity is contagious, BUT so is confidence. I don't know about you, but when I see a confident woman, it inspires me! Let's break the habit of tearing ourselves down and replace it with sharing what makes us beautiful. All we need is a spark to start a wildfire of truly healthy self-esteem. Let's add extra sparkle to the lives around us by being the spark!

In this section, I want to show you all the ways we can be confident and all the ways it pours out of us. It can look like bravery, like Harriet. It can be self-confidence in our appearance. If we nurture that spark, that's when it can spread into the wildfire. Whatever situation you are in, you have the choice to be a beacon of bravery and deep confidence.

If we take a page from Harriet's book, we can see how our actions, our words, and our mindsets can lead others into self-assurance. Let's work on filling ourselves with good, so that is what pours out of us. Let's leave ourselves and others better than how we found them!

- Mckenna

GET INTO IT

Certificate of Victory

YOU have had wins in your life! Let's look back and into the future.

In the chart on the next page, split your life into 3 age categories (they don't have to be exactly even) representing your past, your present, and your future. Ex: If you are 15, you can divide your age into 1-10, 10-15, 15-20.

In each category, think about the wins you've had. What are the successes you've experienced, and what are the successes you would like to have in the future?

Coat of Arms

Have you ever seen an old coat of arms? In Medieval times, knights wore coats of arms (thus wearing their identity) on their sleeves. This told their story because a coat of arms represented who they were, where they were from, their motto, and what they stood for.

So...make your own coat of arms! Fill in the different sections to represent your life. This can be written in words, artistically created, or both! What makes you great? What are you confident in? What do you stand for? The sections can represent what makes you a good sibling, friend, student, athlete, child, or person.

Gratitude Journal

Use the space below to capture all that is in your life that you are grateful for…. pop off any that come to your mind! Write down as many as you can capture.

Go Deeper

1. What are the ways in which you are confident? How could you be more confident?

2. Have you ever been inspired by someone to find your confidence within yourself? What were any takeaways from that experience?

3. Is there someone that comes to mind when you think of a confident woman? Who is that woman, and how are you like them?

You go girl

- [ ] Positive affirmation day! I challenge you to pick a day this week where you choose to give yourself and others only positive affirmations! Whether things go your way or not, whether they go well or poorly, I want you to respond with a positive and forgiving outlook. See how it affects you and those around you.

- [ ] Check out the "Dove Self-Esteem Project" Watch this YouTube video, and see what you think! https://www.youtube.com/watch?v=litXW9IUauE

- [ ] Positive word of the day: this week, each night right before bedtime, capture a positive word about yourself that day. It could be anything - like helpful, kind, smart, resilient, leader.

SECTION FOUR

Competition

This short section will dig into competition and our natural inclination to compare ourselves to one another. How can we be a healthy kind of competitive and learn from each other?

" FILL YOURSELF UP WITH GOOD SO THAT'S WHAT POURS OUT. "

CHAPTER ELEVEN
Competition & Comparison

Let's talk about it

"Real Queens Fix Each Other's Crowns." I love this quote! The visual of girls supporting each other instead of competing against each other is powerful. Oftentimes, in girl world, being mean reigns supreme and competition (girl rivalry) can be cruel. You might not realize it, but there are likely very few times you are not comparing yourself to others – thus, playing a huge part in shaping your identity. You compare your abilities to others as a way of creating a more specific sense of your own identity.

When you believe your own characteristics and traits positively compare to other girls, this can build up your confidence, lessen insecurity and decrease negative competition. However, there is a downside to comparison. If you believe your characteristics and traits negatively compare, it can increase insecurity and create unhealthy competition, which can trigger a "mean girl" mentality toward other girls.

While there exists healthy competition between girls, let's focus on unhealthy comparison and competition because of how destructive they can be in forming your identity.

True or false? You are comparing yourself to others at times when you feel most insecure.
I can confidently say for me, TRUE.

When I was in ninth grade and interested in boys, I was getting ready for a school dance. I wanted to get a new shirt and a cute pair of jeans to hopefully gain the attention of the boy I liked. I remember thinking as I was trying on the jeans, "these jeans make my butt look good– better than they would look on Kenya." And yet, Kenya was one of my best friends.

Then, as I was critiquing the shirt I had tried on, I compared myself to Kenya again, thinking, "she'd look better in this shirt because she has boobs and will fill it out." As I stared in the mirror, all I saw was my flat-as-a-board chest. I couldn't find any shirt I liked because I compared everything I tried on to how it would look on Kenya. From that moment on, I internally competed with Kenya over everything. I was thrilled when a boy she liked chose me. It felt good to "win" at something against her.

Yet, she had no idea we were even in a competition! And, as much as I hate to admit it, I was glad she "lost" for once. As I tried to find my own identity, I ended up developing a huge insecurity about having no chest and almost obsessively compared my chest to all my girlfriends'.

Focusing on what you don't have prevents you from noticing what you do have. When you shift your focus from comparing and negatively competing with other girls to, instead, competing with just yourself and your drive toward your own goals and dreams, you can become better rather than bitter. How do you keep unhealthy competition from taking over your thoughts and dictating your mood and actions? Let's create a new thought process and "reboot" your way of thinking about yourself and other girls.

The author of the book "I'm Happy for You (Sort of...Not Really): Finding Contentment in a Culture of Comparison" shares a mental reboot called **Ctrl+ Alt+ Delete**. This is referenced in the book to reboot in relation to comparison, but since unhealthy comparison leads to unhealthy competition, let's use it for a reboot for negative competition.

Ctrl: Control your thought process. Learn to identify whether competition is positively or negatively affecting you and name it. (We can't fix what we don't know is broken.)

Alt: Alter your perspective on how comparison leads to competition. Take steps to learn how to positively look at yourself. For example, if you struggle with your weight, instead of comparing your body to a friend's, compete against yourself! Challenge yourself to create health-focused goals (P.S., not weight loss-focused goals) to help you feel better about yourself instead of comparing yourself to your friend, which ultimately results in feeling bad about yourself.

Delete: Work to delete the habit of comparing yourself to other girls. Learn to be content with who you are and celebrate your good qualities instead of trying to negatively compete in efforts to be like other girls.

You can admire other girls' beauty, talents, hopes, and

GET INTO IT

Personal Mantras

Create your own personal mantras or statements to repeat to yourself when you struggle with insecurities. I struggle with believing I'm good enough, and sometimes I won't try something out of fear I will fail or fear that I won't be as successful as someone else. Here are two mantras posted in my office to serve as reminders when I begin to compare myself to others. They help me to focus on myself, not them.

"I will speak to my mountains," and
"I feel the fear and move anyway."
In the past, I've also memorized Bible verses and quotes to create my mantras.

Top 10 Affirmations

Magazines have articles focusing on "Top 10's"; "Top 10 Reasons to…" or "Top 10 Ways You…"
Since body image is one of the primary ways girls get sucked into negative girl competition, instead create your own "Top 10 Positive Body Image Affirmations".

Check out my Top 10 on the next page. You can use these, tweak them or create your own! Write them in the mirror you will see on the page that follows.

1. When I compare myself to others, I will remember I look exactly the way I'm supposed to. I know this to be true because this is the way God made me.

2. My body is a temple and needs to be taken care of. I feed my body healthy nourishing food and exercise because it deserves to be taken care of and will keep me stronger.

3. I will be authentically me when others try to dictate who I am or how I look.

4. My body is a yacht for my awesomeness.

5. When I don't feel pretty or don't like the way I look, I will smile. Smiles make other people happy. Making someone else feel better will help me feel better.

6. Just because someone looks perfect on the outside, doesn't mean they have a perfect life. Remember: Don't pre-judge a gift by its wrapping paper.

7. I choose health and healing over diets and punishing myself.

8. Being skinny doesn't make me good. Being fat doesn't make me bad.

9. I can admire other girls and will avoid comparing myself to them.

10. I will appreciate all my body CAN do instead of focusing on what it cannot.

My Top 10 Affirmations

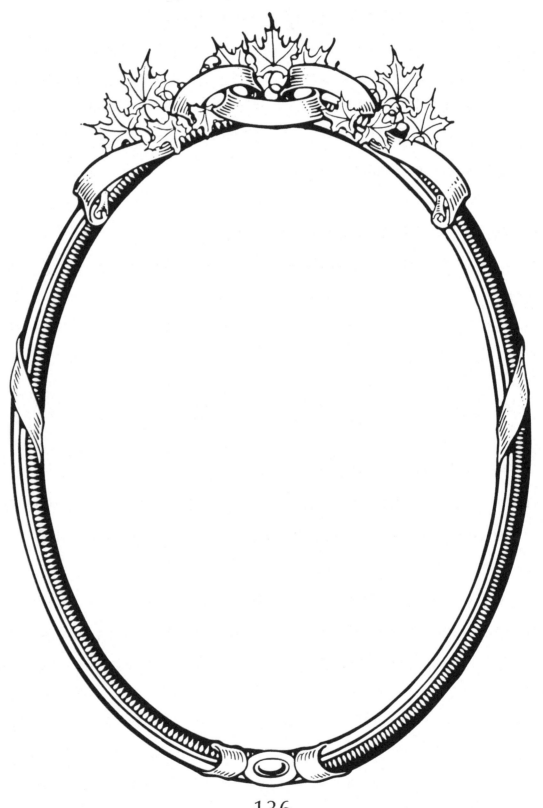

Pump up the Jams

Music is powerful! Listen to these songs or just look up the lyrics and pay attention to the words. Jot down lyrics or songs that stick out to you.

"Beautiful" by Christina Aguilera
Notable lyrics: "You are beautiful, no matter what they say. Words can't bring you down."

"Confident" by Demi Lovato
Notable lyrics: "What's wrong with being confident?"

"Try" by Colbie Caillat
Notable lyrics: "Why should you care what they think of you? When you're all alone, by yourself, do you like you?"

"Scars to Your Beautiful" by Alessia Cara
Notable lyrics: "There's a hope that's waiting for you in the dark. You should know you're beautiful just the way you are.

"Brave" by Sara Bareilles.

Notable Lyrics: "I wonder what would happen if you
Say what you wanna say
And let the words fall out
Honestly I wanna see you be brave."

1. Are you comparing and/or competing with other girls? Is it healthy or unhealthy?

2. Do you compare yourself to other girls when you are most insecure? If so, identify that insecurity.

3. What can you do instead of comparing yourself to other girls when you're feeling insecure?

4. Practice healthy competition. How can I be more kind than my friends?

You go girl

- [ ] Want more girl empowering songs? Head to TMGEP's Playlist on Spotify!

- [ ] Did you write your Top Ten Body Affirmations? Practice saying them in front of the mirror in the morning when you are getting ready or before you go to bed at night.

- [ ] Want to learn more about loving who you are? Check out these books available in most libraries for free or if you want your own, you can get them on Amazon.

- *Embody: Learning to Love Your Unique Body (and Quiet that Critical Voice!)* by Connie Sobczak and Elizabeth Scott (**Amazon**)

- *Mothers, Daughters, and Body Image: Learning to Love Ourselves as We Are* by Hillary L. McBride (**Amazon**)

- *Positive Body Image for Kids: A Strengths-Based Curriculum for Children Aged 7-11* by Ruth Macconville (**Amazon**)

- *The Body is Not an Apology: The Power of Radical Self-Love* by Sonya Renee Taylor (**Amazon**)

- *Body Kindness: Transform Your Health from the Inside Out—and Never Say Diet Again* by Rebecca Scritchfield (**Amazon**)

CHAPTER TWELVE

Social Media

Let's talk about it

The journey to developing your self-identity can be a very vulnerable process, especially during your impressionable teen years! We've talked about how family, culture, and friends can influence you - AND yet, another one of the biggest influences you will face in today's girl world is social media. It can play a critical role in the development of who you are and expose some of your deepest insecurities and comparison issues. Let's address one of them, acceptance. After an assembly I facilitated for The Mean Girl Extinction Project, a group of girls shared how being accepted on social media was as important to them as breathing.

WOW! Such a powerful statement. Their reality was as concerning to me as it was powerful to them. This is why relational aggression (girl bullying) is so prevalent. Girls often harness the power of social media and use it as a weapon to hurt each other because they are very aware of the damage it can cause.

Don't get me wrong - social media can be an awesome tool. It's a cool way to communicate and provide connection. I, too, have felt the pull to be "accepted" on social media. But the reality is, do I choose to hang around people that criticize me and make me feel bad for being who I am? No. So, why should I get sucked up into caring about what those people think of me on social media? AND should I change who I really am because of it? NO!

Apps like Instagram, Snapchat, and TikTok (just to name a few) tend to prey on your insecurities and need for acceptance. If you allow social media to influence your identity based on likes, comments, and views, you are setting yourself up for failure.

Did you know some celebrities have rules that they never read reviews about themselves because there is nothing good that comes of it? The problem is that the desire to be accepted can muddle the difference between who you really are and who you want others to think you are in order to get likes and comments. This can lead to many struggles like stress, anxiety, depression, self-harm, and even suicide.

Your identity needs to be carefully cultivated. So many girls struggle to remember that what you post online is captured literally…forever. Yep! Social media provides a visible and permanent digital record of you. Consider this: Are you being a positive influence on social media, or are you letting it influence you? So, here's the challenge: flip the script with how you use social media. Try to use it as an opportunity to IMPACT others rather than IMPRESS them.

-Shaylene

GET INTO IT

Real or fake?

Scroll through your own feed on one of your social media platforms. Are there any common themes? Does it represent the "real" you or the "fake" you— you know, the one you want others to think you are? Is it a highlight reel, or are you living every moment through social media? Journal about what you discovered.

_____
_____
_____
_____

Social Media Footprint

Who do you follow on social media? Do they encourage you or trigger your insecurities? If they don't encourage you, unfollow them and replace them with people who will make you feel better about yourself! Maybe it's a fitness guru or someone who likes the same hobbies you like.

Design a feed/post that would be encouraging and life- giving!

Go Deeper

1. What do you think about yourself when you don't get a lot of "likes" or comments on a social media post?

2. Do you filter your images on social media to make yourself "look" better? If so, why?

3. Have you ever been cyberbullied? If yes, how did this behavior make you feel?

4. Have you ever cyberbullied another person? If yes, what triggered you to make that choice?

You go girl

- ☐ Pick one of your social media apps. Find someone from your school or social circle and go to their profile. Choose one of their pictures and leave a positive comment.

- ☐ Do something you love. Refrain from taking a picture and posting about it online. Enjoy it! Be present in the moment.

SECTION FIVE

CELEBRATION

You have worked so hard over these past five sections, it's time to throw some confetti for what you've accomplished!

"USE YOUR INFLUENCE TO IMPACT NOT IMPRESS."

YOU DID IT!

YOU DESERVE A CELEBRATION.

If you are reading this, it means you made it to the end of the journal. The intention of this journal was to create a space where you can explore, learn, grow, try things out, process, get creative, relax and add a few tools to your toolbelt. Our hope is that at the end of this journal, you know yourself and how to love and accept who you are a little bit better. From this place of security, our desire is that you would learn to love others with even more passion and intentionality. We are so proud of you. True self-care takes so much energy and intentionality - thank you for giving time to invest in yourself, but let it not stop here.

How well did you do?

This is a perfect time to go back and see how much you accomplished.

Take a few minutes to flip through the pages of this journal and see how many challenge boxes at the end of every chapter you got to check off. If you didn't get to some of them, it's not too late! Challenge yourself to do a few of your unfinished tasks in the coming weeks.

Just one more thing before you go!

You've taken the time to slow down and journey through the journal. As you step away from the pages and close the book, what would it look like to cling to these concepts in your daily life or when you need them most? You have created safety for yourself through the exercises within these pages, and you took the time to dig deep and learn more about your identity.

This safe place between you and yourself will be a place you can cultivate your whole life, but it starts here and now. To create this vibrant and thriving girl world we all dream of, it all starts with acceptance. When you are a beacon of self-acceptance, it champions other women to follow your lead.

When we accept ourselves, we create the space to welcome others into that acceptance. Will there be moments where you will struggle with your identity? Absolutely! So tell yourself what you need to hear when you have forgotten who you are. Let's take a few moments to write this guided letter to yourself.

Throughout these series of journals, this is how they will end, by writing a sealed letter to your future self. Reflecting back on our own words we've written to ourselves can be profound. This letter will be available to you when you struggle or feel like you've lost yourself. When you need it, you will have a letter to open, to help you navigate these feelings. The idea is to create a stacked group of letters for you to open and refer to when you need help, so feel free to remove the letter from the journal and pop it in an envelope!

Follow along with the questions on the following pages, building out your letter to you. The prompts will guide you back over the chapters, gathering highlights from what you've learned.

Dear me,

This is a letter to remind you of who you are. Whatever you are going through, you will be ok, you are never too far gone to come back to yourself. When you doubt this, look to these reflections below, to guide you.

(Page 13-21) When I feel distant from my past, and how I was brought up… I will
_____
_____
_____

(Page 23-32) To have good friends, I need to be a good friend, to be a good friend I will
_____
_____
_____

(Page 33-41) When my femininity is put in a box, I will remember
_____
_____
_____

(Page 43-51) When I need to take my spiritual temperature… I will
_____
_____
_____

(Page 53-64) I will be the best version of myself, this will look like
_____
_____
_____

(Page 143-151) When social media makes me feel insecure I will
_____
_____
_____

(Page 81-91) When my thoughts and emotions feel unsettled, I will
_____
_____
_____

When my world is changing and it's outside of my control, my plan for change will look like (see page 74)
_____
_____
_____

When I'm feeling insecure, I will remember L.O.V.E. (see page 102)
L_____
O_____
V_____
E_____

(Page 115-124) In order to spark confidence in myself, pouring out onto others, I will
_____
_____
_____

When the spirit of unhealthy competition and comparison comes over me, I will remember my "Top 10" (see page 136). They are:
1. _____
2. _____
3. _____
4. _____
5. _____
6. _____
7. _____
8. _____
9. _____
10. _____

open me to remember...

Girl world is tough but so are YOU! You will face battles and when you do, you'll be armed and ready to fight. Say this battle cry with us.

> *"I know who I am. I am uniquely and wonderfully made. I am strong. No one can steal my strength. I have the strength to make others strong."*

YOU matter. We see you, we accept you, and we celebrate you!

love,
Shaylene + Mckenna

& your friends at The Mean Girl Extinction Project

Hotlines

National Suicide Prevention Hotline (24/7): 1.800.273.TALK (1.800.273.8255) [TTY: 1.800.799.4889]	**National Runaway Safeline:** 1.800.RUNAWAY (1.800.786.2929)	**Boystown USA** helping with issues around self-harm, mental health disorders and abuse (24/7): 1.800.448.3000 Or Text VOICE to 20121
Crisis Text Line (24/7): Text SOS to 741741	**National Eating Disorder Association (NEDA) Hotline** (M-Th 11a-9pm EST, Fri 11a-5pm EST): 1.800.931.2237 OR Text NEDA to 741741	**Love is Respect National Teen Dating Abuse Helpline:** 866.331.9474 [TTY: 866.331.8453] Or Text Loveis to 22522
Rape, Abuse & Incest National Network (RAINN) Sexual Assault Hotline: 1.800.656.HOPE (4673)	**Gay Lesbian Transgender National Hotline:** 1.888.843.4564 **LGBTQ Youth Talkline:** 1.800.246.7743	**The Trevor Project- Suicide Prevention and Crisis Intervention for LGBTQ+ youth 13-24:** 1.866.488.7386
Pathways to Safety International- interpersonal and gender-based violence helpline: 1.833.SAFE.833 (723.3833)	**National Human Trafficking Hotline** (24/7): 1.888.373.7888 Or Text HELP or INFO to 233733	**Victim Connect**- for victims of crime: 1.855.4VICTIM (484.2846)
National Alliance on Mental Illness (NAMI) (M-F 10a-6pm EST): 1.800.950.6264	**StrongHearts Native Helpline** (M-F 9a-5:30pm CST): 1.844.7NATIVE (762.8483)	**Add the name and phone number of an adult you trust:**

Additional Resources

Chapter 1: Family & Culture
- Family Tree Genealogy: https://www.familytreemagazine.com/kids-genealogy/
- Tips on how to interview a relative on your family history https://www.familytreemagazine.com/kids/interview
- Here's a powerful way to pull together your family/cultural traditions and history in 1 short document: https://claleadership.org/wp-content/uploads/2021/05/Where-Are-You-From-poem-template.doc.pdf
- YouTube short animated film about differences in family culture: "Me or We?" https://m.youtube.com/watch?v=78haKZhEqcg

Chapter 2: Friends
- Book: "The Friendship Formula" by Kyler Shumway, MA. For girls 12+.
- Book: "The Teen Girl's Survival Guide: Ten Tips for Making Friends, Avoiding Drama, and Coping with Social Stress" by Lucie Hemmen, PHD.

- Book: "The Giving Tree" by Shel Silverstein
- Movie: "Cyberbully" A great example of relational aggression, how it can start out small… and grow to something very toxic.

Chapter 3: Gender Identity:
- Movie: "On the Basis of Sex" - learn about the Notorious RBG, how Ruth Bader Gingsburg defied gender roles for her time! Also book about her for teens: "Dissenter on the Bench", by Victoria Ortiz.
- Girls Equity and Empowerment Resource List https://mcc.gse.harvard.edu/resources-for-educators/girls-equity-and-empowerment-resource-list
- Check out the "Run like a girl" Commercial, by Always. https://m.youtube.com/watch?v=qtDMyGjYlMg
- Movie: "Bend it like Beckham"

Chapter 4: Beliefs
- 10 Cool Meditations for Pre-Teens and Teens https://www.doyou.com/10-cool-meditations-for-pre-teens-and-teens-67578/

- Consider learning about various faith-based beliefs to see what they all have in common. You might be surprised!

Chapter 5: Self
- Self-awareness is key to strengthening your sense of self. Take this quick/easy strengths test to better understand your top strengths high5test.com
- Short animated film: "The reflection of me" about fully accepting yourself. https://m.youtube.com/watch?v=D9OOXCu5XMg

Chapter 6 & 7: Change
- YouTube video "Coping with change" https://m.youtube.com/watch?v=o4yE6BidJCM
- Song "Man in the mirror" by Michael Jackson.
- 99 Coping Skills for Teens: https://www.yourlifeyourvoice.org/journalpages/99-coping-skills-poster.pdf

Chapter 8: Insecurity
- Song "This is me" by Keala Settle.
- Clip "Girls ages 6-18 talk about body image" https://m.youtube.com/watch?v=5mP5RveA_tk

Chapter 9: Prejudice
- Movie: "Glory Road"
- Song: "Where is the Love?" Black Eyed Peas
- Song: "Boys in the Street" Greg Holden
- Quote: "Everybody is a genius. But if you judge a fish by its ability to climb a tree, it will live its whole life believing that it is stupid" - Albert Einstein

Chapter 10: Confidence
- Quote: "You will never speak to anyone more than you speak to yourself in your head. So, play nice".
- Quote: "Comparison is the thief of joy" - Theodore Roosevelt
- Quote: "Remove the 'I want you to like me' sticker from your forehead and place it on the mirror where it belongs". - Susan Jeffers
- Book: "Birdy Brave" by Shaylene King

Chapter 11: Social Media
- Consider following some positive Social Media... check these out: Upworthy, Some Good News, GirlFolkmag, and/or Joshua's Heart Foundation. How many more can you find?
- Quote: "A lie can run around the world before the truth can get it's boots on"- James Watt

Chapter 12: Competition and Comparison

- Words Wound https://wordswound.org/help.php Struggling with bullying? Wish someone could listen and understand? You are not alone! Share your story here. Also a great resource on how to report cyberbullying.
- Movie: "Mean Girls" - a great example of how comparison can impact you and those around you.
- Book: "Liberty Lane and the One-Girl Rebelution", by Shaylene King
- Quote: "And just like accents, we are different, but not wrong."

Pulling it all together... Other General Resources:

- https://www.amightygirl.com/ A must have resource! A Mighty Girl is the world's largest collection of books, toys, movies, and music for girls, parents, teachers, and others dedicated to raising smart, confident, and courageous girls.
- Spotify: Check out our playlist on Spotify! The Mean Girl Extinction Project.
- Book: "Girling up" by Mayim Bialik.

Acknowledgements

From our team:

Girl Tough, Identity is a labor of love from The Mean Girl Extinction Project. Our mission is to help cultivate kindness in girl world.

We believe in the power of words and the importance of using our voices as women to encourage and empower a younger generation of women.
Girl Tough, Identity was co-authored by Shaylene King and Mckenna Stoddart in collaboration with Rhonda Staton, all a part of The Mean Girl Extinction Project organization.

We know girl bullying can result from insecurities that are often tied to one's identity. When you understand who you are as a girl and create health and security around your identity, you will be less likely to mistreat other girls and more likely to cultivate kindness in girl world. Thank you for helping us continue our mission to cultivate kindness in girl world through this journal.

We would like to give our sincerest gratitude to the William H. Donner Foundation Inc., which funded the grant to write and publish Girl Tough, Identity. Without the William H. Donner Foundation Inc., this project would not have been possible.

From Shaylene King:

As founder of The Mean Girl Extinction Project, I would first like to thank Rhonda Staton, who has been with The Mean Girl Extinction Project from conception. I am so thankful for your wisdom around all things non-profit, as well as your ability to reign in my BIG dreams to purposeful bite-sized pieces. Thank you for your contribution to this project. Your input provided valuable checks and balances to ensure our content for this journal was well-rounded and met the project's objectives.

Thank you, Mckenna, for co-writing this book with me. You had no idea what you were walking into when I asked you to be a part of this project, yet you jumped right in. Thank you for trusting me with your words. It's been dreamy to write this book with you.

You're a beautiful gift to The Mean Girl Extinction Project, and your love for girls and desire for them to love themselves and thrive is captivating to watch and an honor to stand alongside you to serve.

There are so many people I would love to acknowledge personally, but the list would be never-ending to name them one by one. So, suffice it to say, I am eternally thankful for my husband Mike, who has believed in me and encouraged my every dream, including The Mean Girl Extinction Project. The tribe of women in my life who help support me as I navigate girl world. They cheer me on and celebrate life's wins and hold me up when life's losses are hard. They pray with me and for me. Ethan and Jordan, thank you for the sacrifices you made all those years ago when I decided to start The Mean Girl Extinction Project. I am a better woman because God allowed me to be your mom. Above all, I'm thankful to the Lord who has called me to be a voice for all girls and to help them find their voice.

From Mckenna Stoddart:

It has been a privilege to pour out my heart and mind in this Journal, and I owe that privilege to Shaylene King.

Shay, thank you for believing in me and inviting me to join you on this creative adventure. You have led this project so well, and your passion to help young women inspires me.

I want to thank the one that sparked my love and desire to be in close a community with young women, Marta Grillenzoni. Friendship with you has been a blessing to me.

My heart abounds in gratitude to the community that has shaped me. Firstly, to my parents, Julie and Darrin Jones, who taught me everything I know about loving yourself and loving others. To my brother Sawyer, close friends from Biola, and the Sunshine Coast friends and family, for refining me as a person and supporting me. Finally, to my husband Caleb for championing me through every challenge, encouraging me, and for the hours he volunteered to help develop this journal. None of this would have been possible without the power of prayer and guidance from the Lord, who gave me a heart for girls and to see them reach their full potential.

About the Authors

Shaylene is the founder of The Mean Girl Extinction Project, a 501(c)3 non-profit created to address the rise in relational aggression among girls. She teaches girls how to not only survive girl world but to make a difference and thrive in girl world. Shaylene also teaches and trains the nation's leading student-led bully prevention program, Safe School Ambassadors.

She works to equip students with the tools they need to develop self-confidence while practicing and promoting positive communication with their peers.

Shaylene lives with her husband in Middle Tennessee, sailing the unchartered waters of empty nesting. She enjoys any time she gets to spend with her two grown children who are off exploring the world and living the life God created for them.

Mckenna is the Vice President of The Mean Girl Extinction Project. She is a graduate of Biola University, where she studied sociology and fell in love with mental health. She worked as a Residential Advisor where she discovered her passion for championing the women alongside her to be their most authentically healthy selves.

Mckenna had the opportunity to teach middle schoolers while briefly living in Italy, where her heart found a soft spot for middle and high school young women. She now works for Golden Goose Consulting as a certified Life Coach, journeying with and empowering others.

Mckenna lives in Australia, on the Sunshine Coast with her Aussie husband Caleb and their cat, London. While her family lives in Tennessee, she explores this season of cross-cultural living. She loves enjoying all the adventures, beauty, and coffee that their little beach town has to offer.

Contributors

Rhonda Staton is a Licensed Clinical Social Worker who earned her master's degree in Social Welfare from UC Berkeley. She has decades of hands-on and leadership experience working with and advocating for at-risk and disadvantaged populations such as current and former foster youth, individuals with brain injuries, adults with mental illness, and homeless veterans. Ms. Staton has volunteered as a sexual assault counselor and has been the responder on various crisis hotlines, including the National Suicide Hotline, a grief hotline, homeless hotlines, and a school tip line. She has either volunteered or been employed in a non-profit setting for over 30 years. She has experience in grant writing for non-profits securing funds for small events to multi-year contracts with County or other governmental agencies.

We hope you loved your journey through this Girl Tough, Identity journal as much as we loved writing it for you!

And— while we're on the topic of you, TMGEP has some freebies created just for you! Head over to The Mean Girl Extinction Project at tmgep.com. Once there you will find our Girl Tough page, where you can download FREE notecards of some quotes you saw in this journal, as well as some wallpapers for your desktop and/or phone.

Be on the lookout for our next Girl Tough journal. We can't wait to share it with you! And, so you don't miss the announcement of our next Girl Tough journal, the cover reveal, or the launch date, you can subscribe at tmgep.com and/or follow us on our social media platforms.

See you there!

Made in the USA
Columbia, SC
28 September 2022